D0471466

THE HISTORY OF THE CLEVELAND BROWNS

THE HISTORY OF THE
CLEVELAND

Published by Creative Education
123 South Broad Street
Mankato, Minnesota 56001
Creative Education is an imprint of The Creative Company.

DESIGN AND PRODUCTION BY **EVANSDAY DESIGN**

Copyright © 2005 Creative Education.
International copyright reserved in all countries.
No part of this book may be reproduced in any form
without written permission from the publisher.
Printed in the United States of America

LIBRARY OF CONGRESS CATALOGING-IN-PUBLICATION DATA

Gilbert, Sara.
The history of the Cleveland Browns / by Sara Gilbert.
p. cm. — (NFL today)
Summary: Traces the history of the team from its beginnings through 2003.
ISBN 1-58341-293-X
1. Cleveland Browns (Football team : 1999)—History—Juvenile literature.
[1. Cleveland Browns (Football team : 1999)—History. 2. Football—History.]
I. Title. II. Series.

GV956.C6F74 2004
796.332'64'0977132—dc22   2003065040

First edition

9 8 7 6 5 4 3 2 1

COVER PHOTO: defensive end Courtney Brown

PHOTOGRAPHS BY
AP/Wide World Photos, Corbis (Bettmann, Reuters), Getty Images

Sara Gilbert

3 1730 06336 0601

CLEVELAND, OHIO, IS A BUSY PORT CITY THAT SITS ALONG THE SHORE OF LAKE ERIE. LONG KNOWN AS A HARDWORKING, INDUSTRIAL CITY, CLEVELAND HAS UNDERGONE A MAJOR TRANSFORMATION IN RECENT YEARS AND IS TODAY A MODERN-LOOKING METROPOLIS OF ALMOST 500,000 PEOPLE. BRINGING IN THOUSANDS OF VISITORS EACH YEAR, CLEVELAND BOASTS SUCH ATTRACTIONS AS THE ROCK AND ROLL HALL OF FAME AND THE CLEVELAND METROPARK ZOOS. OVER THE YEARS, MANY PEOPLE HAVE ALSO COME TO CLEVELAND TO WATCH ITS PROFESSIONAL FOOTBALL TEAM. SINCE THE CLUB KNOWN AS THE BROWNS CAME TO TOWN AS A MEMBER OF THE ALL-AMERICA FOOTBALL CONFERENCE (AAFC) IN 1946, IT HAS BEEN REVERED AS AN OHIO INSTITUTION. OVER THE COURSE OF A LONG AND SUCCESSFUL HISTORY IN THE NATIONAL FOOTBALL LEAGUE (NFL), THE BROWNS HAVE BUILT A REPUTATION FOR BEING AS HARDWORKING AND LOYAL AS THE FANS WHO SUPPORT THEM.

[1964 Cleveland Browns]

THE ORIGINAL BROWN>

CLEVELAND'S PRO FOOTBALL tradition took root when team owner Arthur McBride picked Paul Brown— an Ohio native who led Ohio State University to a national college championship in 1942—to lead his new AAFC club. The city of Cleveland applauded that choice by picking the popular coach's last name in a "name-the-team" contest, and the Cleveland Browns were born.

The Browns emerged as the AAFC's most fearsome team. With quarterback Otto Graham, fullback Marion Motley, and offensive tackle and place kicker Lou "the Toe" Groza leading the charge, the Browns compiled a 52–4–3 record in the league's four-year history and won all four championships. Still, few people believed the Browns could continue that success in the NFL when the AAFC folded in 1949.

At 230 pounds, fullback Marion Motley was tough to stop.^

Coach Brown believed. And when his team defeated the defending NFL champion Philadelphia Eagles 35–10 in the first game of the 1950 season, everyone else began to believe, too. "Coach Brown should have been a general," Graham said after the game. "For four years, we had been hearing how we were inferior to NFL teams. During that time, Coach Brown didn't say one word. He would just cut out all these clippings and put them on the bulletin board. I assure you, when we finally played Philadelphia, there was never a team in the history of sports that was more emotionally ready to play a game."

The 1950 Browns proved just how good they were by going 10–2 and winning the NFL championship. With the help of defensive end Len Ford, center Frank Gatski, and receiver Dante Lavelli, Cleveland went on to win the NFL Eastern Division title six years in a row, capturing two more league championships in 1954 and 1955. In the 1954 championship game against the Detroit Lions, Graham threw for three touchdowns and ran for three more. In 1955, he led the team to a 38–14 victory over the Los Angeles Rams.

That was the last professional game for Graham, who decided to retire while he was on top. Almost half a century has passed since Coach Brown called the Hall-of-Famer "the greatest ever to play the

ANOTHER GREAT BROWN>

GRAHAM'S DEPARTURE OPENED the door for a new superstar in Cleveland: running back Jim Brown, a 6-foot-2 and 230-pound powerhouse drafted by the Browns in 1957. With a frightening combination of speed and strength, Brown wasted no time in rising to stardom. In 1957, he ran for 942 yards, scored nine touchdowns, and was named Rookie of the Year. The following year, he nearly doubled those numbers. Before the end of his NFL career, Brown would gain 12,312 total yards, score 126 touchdowns, and win an incredible eight league rushing titles.

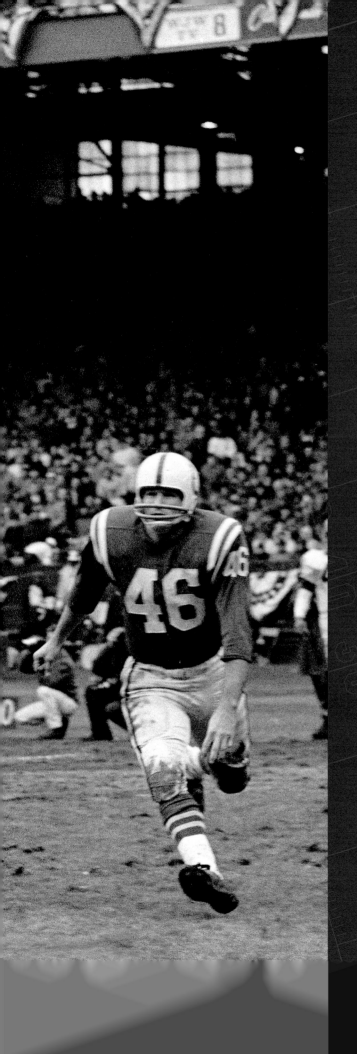

With offensive tackle Mike McCormack and wide receiver Gary Collins also wearing Cleveland brown and orange, the Browns put together a string of winning seasons that culminated in a trip to the NFL championship game in 1964. Under new coach Blanton Collier, they defeated the Baltimore Colts 27–0 for their fourth NFL championship.

In 1965, Brown had another stunning season, rushing for more than 1,500 yards and winning NFL Most Valuable Player (MVP) honors. But after Cleveland lost to the Green Bay Packers in the NFL championship game, he surprised the sports world by retiring at the age of 30. Brown left the game as the NFL's all-time leading rusher; more than two decades would pass before his yardage record would be broken by Chicago Bears great Walton Payton. "It is possible that had Brown continued to play, he would have put all the league's rushing records so far out of reach that they would have been only a distant dream…to the runners who followed him," noted *Sports Illustrated* writer Peter King.

Brown's retirement slowed Cleveland's running attack only temporarily. Leroy Kelly quickly proved to be a quality replacement as he lined up behind talented quarterbacks Frank Ryan and Bill Nelsen. These players carried the Browns back to the NFL championship game in 1968 and 1969, but the Browns lost both times.

When the American Football League merged with the NFL in 1970, the Browns were moved to the Central Division of the new American Football Conference (AFC). Despite the best efforts of running back Greg Pruitt and wide receiver Paul Warfield, the Browns played inconsistently, making the playoffs only twice during the decade.

SIPE AND THE KARDIAC KIDS>

HOPE RETURNED TO Cleveland when coach Forrest Gregg promoted backup quarterback Brian Sipe to the starting lineup in 1976. The Browns went 6–8 in 1977, then 8–8 in 1978. By 1980, Sipe and the Browns had earned a reputation as a team capable of amazing last-minute heroics. After winning seven games in dramatic fashion that season, fans began referring to the club as the "Kardiac Kids."

The Browns had plenty of talent during that 1980 season, including Pruitt, tight end Ozzie Newsome, and defensive end Lyle Alzado. But no one played better than Sipe, who threw for more than 4,000 yards and 30 touchdowns—efforts that earned him the NFL MVP award. "He's a winner, and I think that just says it all in a whole," said Newsome, Cleveland's all-time pass receptions leader. "He does whatever he thinks it takes for us to win the game."

During a 13-year Browns career, Ozzie Newsome made more catches (662) than any tight end in history.

The 1980 Browns won the AFC Central with an 11–5 record, earning home-field advantage in the playoffs. Any AFC team hoping to reach the Super Bowl would have to survive the cold and wind of Cleveland Municipal Stadium—and then manage to get past the Kardiac Kids. In the first round of the playoffs, the Oakland Raiders came to town hoping to do just that.

With the Browns behind 14–12 late in the game and deep in Raiders territory, Sipe dropped back to pass. Under pressure, he scrambled, almost fell, and then threw. Unfortunately, the ball sailed right into the hands of Oakland safety Mike Davis, and the Raiders won the game and went on to claim the Super Bowl.

That loss seemed to take the heart out of the Kardiac Kids. Sipe left Cleveland in 1983, and a year later the team made a head coaching change, bringing in Marty Schottenheimer. Coach Schottenheimer and the Browns then started looking for their next star.

THE BROWNS FOUND that star in their own backyard. Bernie Kosar had grown up near Cleveland and made it clear that he wanted to return to his home state to play professionally after his college career at the University of Miami. The Browns, impressed by the young quarterback's leadership and strong arm, selected Kosar in the 1985 NFL Draft.

With Kosar firing the ball to a trio of sure-handed targets—Newsome, Webster Slaughter, and Brian Brennan— the 1986 Browns fought to a 12–4 record. With their team once again having home-field advantage in the playoffs, Cleveland fans were confident that this was finally their year.

Star quarterback Bernie Kosar was one of eight Browns players elected to the Pro Bowl in 1987.

In the first round of the playoffs, the Browns fell behind the New York Jets. Late in the game, Jets defensive lineman Mark Gastineau slammed into Kosar well after he had released the ball. Kosar got up more determined than ever to rally the Browns. "I saw a look in his eyes I'd never seen before," Newsome recalled. "He was not going to be denied. He was going to find a way to win that football game."

Kosar and the Browns did find a way, scoring twice to force sudden-death overtime, then booting a field goal to win 23–20. But the team's luck ran out a week later when it faced the Denver Broncos in the AFC championship game. Although the Browns held a 20–13 lead late in the fourth quarter, Denver quarterback John Elway led the Broncos to a last-minute tying score and then a 23–20 overtime victory. The 80,000 fans in Municipal Stadium went home broken-hearted once again.

The Browns had a chance again in 1987, when they won their division and advanced to the AFC title game to again take on the Broncos. Cleveland trailed by 21 in the third quarter before Kosar engineered three scoring drives to tie the game at 31–31. After Denver scored another touchdown, Kosar had his team on the move deep in Denver territory. Sadly, a fumble near the goal line shattered the Browns' Super Bowl dreams again.

Cleveland remained an AFC powerhouse in the seasons that followed. In 1989, the Browns again faced Denver in the conference title game—and again, they lost. That closed the door on a decade that was both thrilling and frustrating. Then, in spite of the fierce play of linebacker Clay Matthews and defensive end Michael Dean Perry, the Browns opened the 1990s with four straight losing seasons. In 1993, the team's fans bid a sad farewell when Kosar was traded away. Little did they know that the worst was yet to come.

THE BROWNS BEGIN AGAIN>

EVEN DURING THE losing seasons of the early 1990s, Browns fans packed the seats at Cleveland Municipal Stadium, especially the end-zone home of the "Dawg Pound," a group of face-painting and mask-wearing fans known for their especially rowdy cheering. So when team owner Art Modell announced in 1995 that he was moving the franchise to Baltimore, Maryland, because aging Municipal Stadium wasn't generating enough money, the fans were devastated.

But the city refused to accept that this was the end. Cleveland immediately filed a lawsuit on behalf of the fans, forcing the NFL to negotiate with Cleveland's mayor. The city retained the proud Browns name, colors, and history. It also received a promise that the NFL would help fund a new stadium and bring a team back to Cleveland by 1999.

Ownership of the new team was granted to Al
Lerner, a local banker, and Carmen Policy, a former
San Francisco 49ers team official. As Municipal
Stadium was demolished and the new Cleveland
Browns Stadium was built on the same site, Lerner
and Policy hired offense-minded coach Chris Palmer
as the team's sidelines leader. One of Coach Palmer's
first tasks was to develop the club's top pick in the
1999 NFL Draft, quarterback Tim Couch.

It would be a long road for Couch and his team-
mates. When the new Browns took the field for
their first game in 1999, they were crushed 43–0 by
the Pittsburgh Steelers. More than a month would
go by before the team recorded its first victory,
a 21–16 triumph over the New Orleans Saints in
the Louisiana Superdome. But Couch's late-game
heroics that afternoon renewed the team's hopes
for the future.

The Browns were behind by two points with 21
seconds left in the game when Couch launched a
56-yard, "Hail Mary" pass that came down in the
arms of Browns receiver Kevin Johnson for the winning touchdown. "It's a memory I'll never forget,"
Couch said. "I can remember [New Orleans coach]
Mike Ditka laying on the carpet and seeing him as
I was running down the sideline. That was prob-
ably the best part of all."

The foundation of the new Browns' rebuilding efforts, Tim Couch showed poise under pressure.

Down! Touch 29 Set! Hut Hut!

Kevin Johnson sprint from Seattle in a Browns victory

After the Browns finished 1999 with a 2–14 record, they steadily improved, jumping to 3–13 in 2000 and 7–9 in 2001. By 2002, the team had a balanced mix of young players such as Couch, Johnson, defensive end Courtney Brown, and powerful running back William Green; and veterans such as safety Robert Griffith and offensive lineman Ross Verba. Behind these players, the Browns surged back into the playoffs with a 9–7 mark. The team stumbled in 2003, but the addition of veteran quarterback Jeff Garcia in 2004 promised to help Cleveland rebound again.

The Cleveland Browns have been building a tradition of excellence in the Midwest for more than half a century. During those decades, the team has captured four NFL championships and had 13 players earn a place in the Pro Football Hall of Fame. With today's "new" Browns showing the same hardworking attitude that made the Browns of yesterday great, Cleveland hopes to soon add "NFL champions" to its list of attractions.

INDEX>